THIRTY TRILLION CELLS

HOW YOUR BODY REALLY WORKS

Written by Isabel Thomas

Illustrated by Dawn Cooper

W

WELBECK
EDITIONS

Published in 2022 by Welbeck Editions
An Imprint of Welbeck Children's Limited, part of Welbeck Publishing Group.
Offices in: London - 20 Mortimer Street, London W1T 3JW &
Sydney - Level 17, 207 Kent St, Sydney NSW 2000 Australia
www.welbeckpublishing.com

Art Editor: Deborah Vickers
Designer: Kathryn Davies
Associate Publisher: Laura Knowles
Editor: Jenni Lazell

ISBN 978-1-80338-017-9

Printed in Heshan, China
10 9 8 7 6 5 4 3 2 1

FSC
www.fsc.org
MIX
Paper | Supporting
responsible forestry
FSC® C020056

CONTENTS

CELLS ARE THE BUILDING BLOCKS OF YOU!

Everything is made of atoms. These tiny particles are the building blocks of rocks and rockets, cars and clouds . . . and of living things like you. But rocks don't move like you do, cars can't grow like you, do and clouds never eat or breathe like you do. If everything is made from atoms, what makes living things so different?

The answer is CELLS.

All living things—from trees to tigers to tiny microbes—are made up of one or more cells. Cells are the real building blocks of life. A cell is **MUCH BIGGER** than an atom. In fact, there are about 100 trillion atoms packed into a typical cell. But cells are still tiny compared to you. Most cells can only be seen with the help of a microscope.

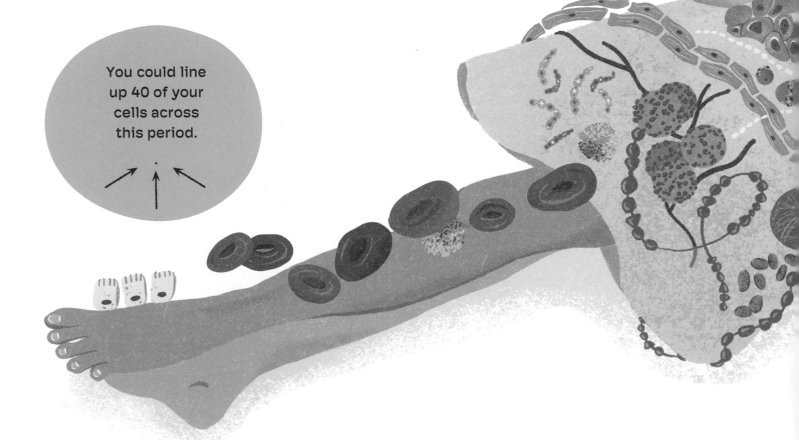

You could line up 40 of your cells across this period.

It takes about 30 trillion (30,000,000,000,000) cells to build your body. Despite their micro size, your cells aren't identical blobs or bricks. There are many different types of human cells, of different shapes and sizes. Each one is packed with the materials and machinery of life and is busy doing certain jobs. Each cell is also busy sharing messages and materials with the other cells in your body—working together to help you move, grow, eat, sense, and react to the world around you.

Your body is also home to more than 30 trillion cells that aren't human! Find out more about your mysterious microbe helpers in chapter five.

By **understanding your cells**,
you can better understand . . .

. . . how your body works
. . . why you grow and develop in a certain way
. . . what happens when you get ill
. . . how your body repairs itself
. . . and who you are.

Your cells are **complicated, fascinating and beautiful— 30 trillion tiny pieces of you.**
Let's get to know them better.

Chapter 1

WHAT'S INSIDE A CELL?

Cells are the smallest working parts of a living thing. Plants and animals—including humans—are made up of billions or trillions of cells. But many living things are made up of just one cell.

Each living cell is like a room with a wall. This wall (called a membrane) is very important. It controls what comes in and out of the cell. It lets the cell gather different chemicals together in one place and keep conditions on the inside of the cell very different from conditions outside. These two facts mean that:

- a cell can break down chemicals to release energy
- a cell can make new chemicals called proteins.

Human cells can make at least 20,000 different proteins (not all at once!). These proteins carry out all the different jobs in your body.

Cell zones

A cell is very crowded! But it's also very organized. Cells are divided up into many different zones, with different "machinery" for gathering, arranging, breaking down, building, organizing, and transporting chemicals. If you could walk into one of your cells, here are some of the main zones you could visit . . .

To do all these things, cells use energy—lots of it. **Mitochondria** are the powerhouses of your cells, breaking down fats and sugars to release energy.

Ribosomes are little factories where proteins are made.

The **membrane** keeps the squishy insides together. It lets in things the cell needs and keeps out things that could harm the cell.

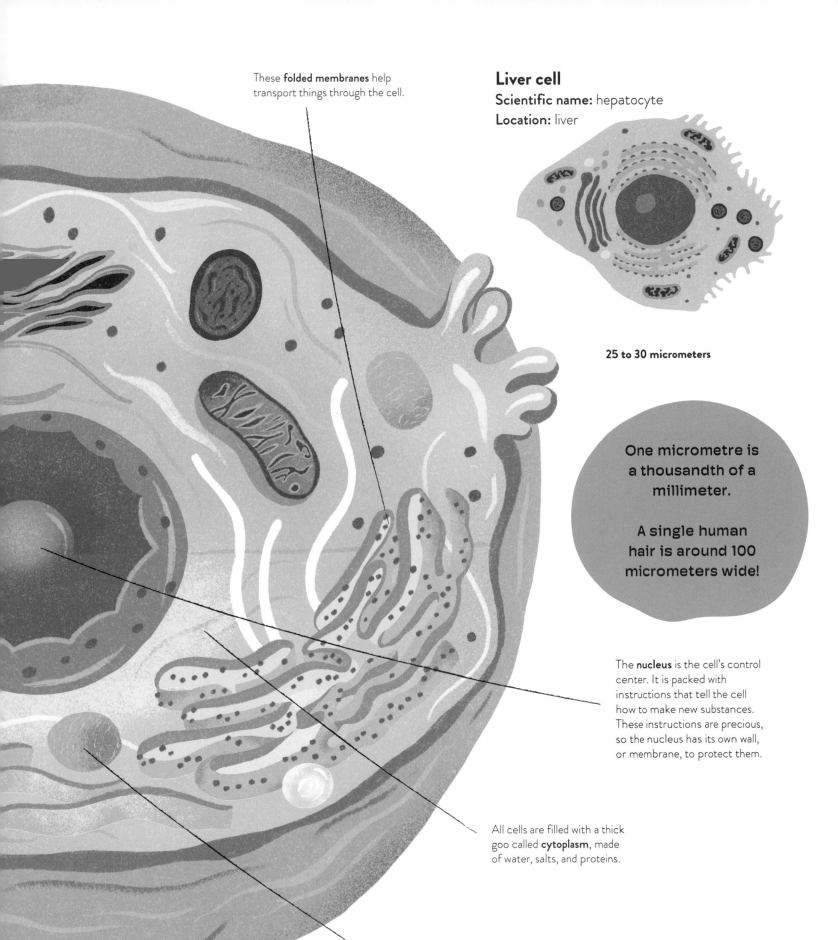

These **folded membranes** help transport things through the cell.

Liver cell
Scientific name: hepatocyte
Location: liver

25 to 30 micrometers

One micrometre is a thousandth of a millimeter.

A single human hair is around 100 micrometers wide!

The **nucleus** is the cell's control center. It is packed with instructions that tell the cell how to make new substances. These instructions are precious, so the nucleus has its own wall, or membrane, to protect them.

All cells are filled with a thick goo called **cytoplasm**, made of water, salts, and proteins.

These little **sacs** (vacuoles) store substances until they are needed.

WHY DO WE HAVE SO MANY CELLS?

Cells are complicated! A creature made of just one cell—such as an amoeba—has everything it needs to move, feed, get rid of waste, grow, sense, react, and reproduce. But if one cell can do everything needed to stay alive, what's the point of having more than one cell? Why do humans need 30 trillion cells?

It's a tough world out there. Every day, living things compete to find food and avoid getting eaten. Teaming up can really help their chances. Amoebas usually live on their own as single cells. But when conditions get tough, some types of amoebas group together to form a big blob known as a slime mold. Together, the slime mold can creep across the forest floor much faster and farther than a single amoeba could go on its own, vacuuming up all sorts of food. Each cell communicates with the others using chemical signals.

Bone cells

Dog vomit slime mold
(*Fuligo septica*)

Your body is also a collection of cells that work together to give them all a better chance of survival. But it's not just a supersize version of the dog vomit slime mold, where every cell is the same. Your body is made up of more than 200 different types of cells. They have very different shapes and sizes and behave differently too.

Super specialists

Most of your body cells don't have what it takes to survive on their own. They have lost the ability to do certain jobs so that they can become better at others. For example, fat cells have given up all their organelles so they can store more fat. Red blood cells have no nucleus so they can carry as much oxygen as possible. Individually your cells are less streetwise than an amoeba, but they communicate and share resources so well with each other that it doesn't matter.

By working together, they form the most complex organism on the planet—YOU! (No amoeba has ever painted a picture, written a book, invented a space rocket, or beaten the Ender Dragon).

Brain cells

Heart cells

Skin cells

But there is still one big question: how does each of your **30 trillion cells** know which **type of cell to be?**

HOW DO CELLS KNOW WHAT TO DO?

Most cells in your body are specialized. They are only good at doing one job. If your muscle cells were replaced with brain cells, your muscles would not work, and vice versa. How does each cell know what to do? And how did it know which type of cell to be in the first place?

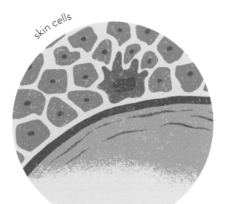

skin cells

The main thing that all cells do is build complicated chemicals called proteins. Those proteins carry out different jobs. The instructions for building proteins are found in the cell's control center, or nucleus. Let's zoom in to the nucleus of a skin cell. If you magnify it about 1,000 times, you can see tiny strands called chromosomes. There are 46 chromosomes in every human cell.

Building blocks

Zoom in to a chromosome, and you see that it's made of a chemical called deoxyribonucleic acid (DNA for short). The building blocks of DNA are called bases. There are four types of bases, arranged in very long chains like beads on a bracelet. The order of the bases turns out to be a code—for making proteins! Cells can read the DNA code, then use it to assemble the building blocks of proteins in the right order.

Instruction manual

Most cells in your body contain the entire DNA code for making at least 20,000 kinds of human proteins—the complete set of instructions on how to build a human! This instruction manual is known as a genome. But a cell will only read the instructions to make the proteins it needs to do its job—as a skin cell, a heart cell, a nerve cell, or a muscle cell. It's as if all the other pages of the instruction manual have been glued together so they can't be read!

A genome is not a fixed set of instructions like a LEGO manual. It is more like a recipe book, where cells can pick and choose the instructions they need at the time. This is why your environment—all the things you eat, learn, hear, see, and experience as you grow up—are just as important as your genome in shaping who you become.

The section of DNA that tells a cell how to make one particular protein is called a gene.

Chapter 2

BRAIN CELLS

Human cells always work in teams. Similar cells team up in large numbers to form tissues. Different tissues team up to form organs that work together to build a certain part of your body. Your brain is the most complicated organ of all.

The control center

The brain is more complex than the world's most powerful computers—which makes sense because human brains designed those computers, but computers can't design and build human brains!

There are thousands of different types of "brain cells." Each one is busy working on its own projects, and together they act as your control center. They collect a huge amount of information from inside your body and from the outside world, then tell every cell in your body how to respond.

You've got a lot of nerve

Nerve cells are the main building blocks of your brain—and the rest of your nervous system (*see pages 44–45*). They are constantly communicating with each other using electrical signals. These are passed on through the long "fingers" that stick out of each nerve cell. They make connections with other nerve cells, like a living version of the Internet.

If you look closely at a brain cell, you'll notice two types of these spindly "fingers." The first are dendrites, which collect electrical signals from other cells. Some cells have lots of dendrites. The second type are axons. A nerve cell usually has one axon, which carries away electrical signals made by that cell.

Building pathways

There are more than a trillion connections between the nerve cells in your brain! So the number of different pathways a nerve signal can take is almost infinite. Whenever you learn something new, a brand-new pathway is created. When you recall it, nerve signals zip along that same pathway again.

Essential workers

Fewer than half your brain cells are nerve cells. There is also a huge team of glial cells, which do all the jobs needed to keep the nerve cells working properly. They are your brain's janitors, scaffolders, litter pickers, soldiers, doctors, and electricians!

Some glial cells repair damage and get rid of anything that shouldn't be in your brain (such as germs or parts of old, dead cells). Others act like the coating on the electrical cords in your home, wrapping themselves around nerve cells so their electrical signals don't leak out in the wrong places.

At first, scientists thought glial cells were just "glue" between nerve cells. Today we know they play all kinds of important roles in the brain.

Nerve cells
Scientific name: neurons
Location: your brain and nervous system

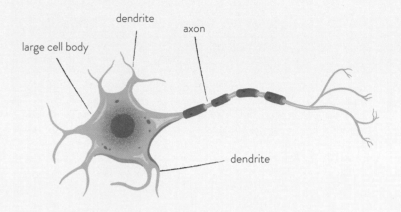

large cell body

dendrite

axon

dendrite

The largest nerve cells have processes that reach from the bottom of your spine to the tips of your toes.

Support cells
Scientific name: glial cells
Location: your brain and nervous system

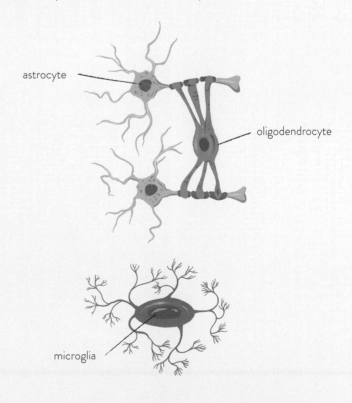

astrocyte

oligodendrocyte

microglia

Astrocyte cell bodies are 10–20 micrometers across, meaning you could line up 10 across a single human hair.

13

HEART CELLS

Your heart may be your hardest-working organ! Brain cells get a chance to rest and repair themselves while you sleep, but your heart never takes a break. How do heart cells do it?

Your heart is a much simpler organ than your brain. It has just one job to do, which is to pump blood around your body. Around 11 different types of cells help get this job done. The main type are heart muscle cells.

Pump up the action

Your heart is about the size of your clenched fist, and you can use your fists to find out how it works. Cup your hands in a bowl of water. Squeeze your palms together, and you'll see water squirt up into the air. Your hands are acting as a pump. Your heart works in a similar way, but with three big differences:

1) Your heart is really two pumps side by side.
2) These pumps are much more powerful than the one you made with your fists.
3) Your brain told your hands to squeeze together, but your heart doesn't rely on your brain to tell it what to do.

Heart muscle cells are packed with more mitochondria than most cells have. These extra "powerhouses" convert energy from your food into energy that cells can use to help your heart work nonstop, without getting tired.

Heart muscle cells provide the pushing force that gets blood moving.

Changing chambers

Your heart is made up of four hollow chambers with thick, muscly walls. Heart muscle cells are the main building blocks of these walls. They contract (get shorter) and then relax (get longer) in time with each other. Two hundred million of these cells are packed into every dice-size section of your heart wall! When these cells all contract at the same time, they cause the walls of your heart to change shape, pushing blood through your body.

Heart muscle cells

Scientific name: cardiomyocytes
Location: your heart walls

cylinder-shaped

contract when they get an electrical signal

relax when the electrical signal fades

100–150 micrometers long

Heart pacemaker cells

Scientific name: sinoatrial node cells
Location: a patch of wall of the top right chamber of your heart

smaller than other heart muscle cells

sends electrical signals out in a regular rhythm, about 100 times a minute

can make their own electrical signals like a nerve cell can

100–150 micrometers long

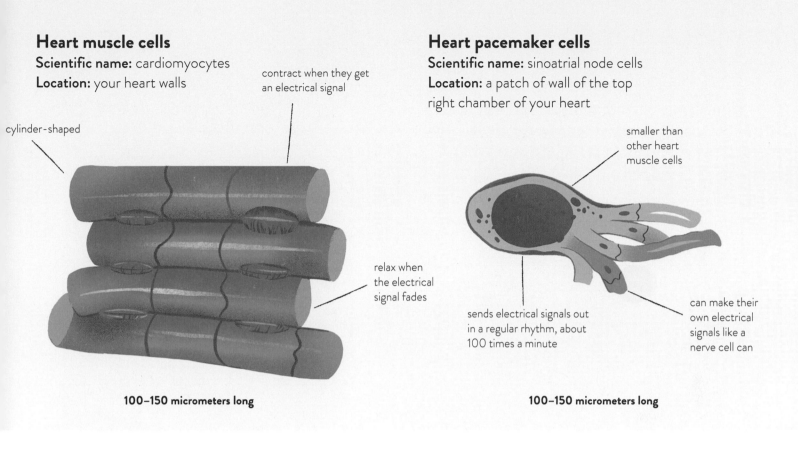

Building a heart

For a heart to work properly, other types of cells and tissues are needed too. These include blood cells that build the tough, grisly "skeleton" of your heart and keep valves and blood vessels firmly attached.

Hearts cells are not very good at repairing and replacing themselves. By the time someone is 50 years old, more than half of their heart cells are the same ones they had when they were born. Eating healthily and exercising often keeps them working well.

Keep the beat

Heart muscle cells react to electrical signals, which come from "pacemaker" cells in the heart itself. We have about 10,000 of these special cells, and they are all clustered in one patch that is less than one inch across.

Your brain is not in charge of your heartbeat, but it is pretty bossy and constantly changes the rate! When you exercise, get a fright, or feel stressed, your brain releases chemicals into your blood that speed up your heart rate—making you ready for action.

Each squeeze and release is one heartbeat. Your heart beats around once every second when you are resting, which adds up to at least three billion beats during a lifetime.

FAT CELLS

For a long time, we thought that fat cells were just tiny warehouses that stored fat. Now we've discovered they are secretly in control of your appetite, your blood sugar levels, and even how active your immune system is!

Fats are so important that your body has special cells dedicated to storing them. Fat cells are like balloons that can fill themselves up with lipids, swelling to many times their original size. Fat is a fantastic store of energy. When your body needs extra energy (because you haven't eaten for a long time or because you are exercising) your fat cells convert some of their stored fat into fuel for your muscles.

Adipose, I suppose

Fat cells cluster together to form adipose tissue. Most of this soft, squishy tissue is found in a layer just below your skin, where it traps body heat and helps keep you warm. Fat tissue is also found between the different organs in your body, where it acts like a cushion to keep organs from bumping into each other and getting damaged as you move around. The pads under your heels are made of adipose tissue. There is a thick layer of it in each buttock. There is even a cushion of fat around your eyes. Fat is like Bubble Wrap for your body!

Every ounce of adipose tissue contains up to 57 million fat cells.

White, brown, and beige

We all have three different types of fat cells:

White fat cells	Brown fat cells	Beige fat cells
White fat cells convert sugars and proteins into fat and store it, ready for when you need that energy boost.	These cells burn fat in a way that releases energy as heat and warms us up. Babies have lots of brown fat cells. In adult humans they are found in only a few parts of the body.	White fat cells can turn into a third type of fat cells, known as beige fat cells. These act like brown fat cells but can be found all around the body.

White fat cells

Scientific name: white adipocytes

Location: around organs and just under the skin

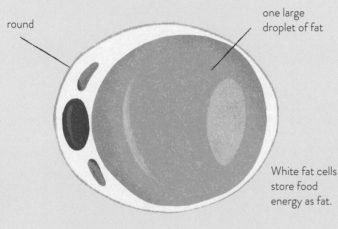

round

one large droplet of fat

White fat cells store food energy as fat.

up to 150 micrometers when they are full of fat

Brown fat cells

Scientific name: brown adipocytes

Location: between your shoulder blades and around your neck and collarbone

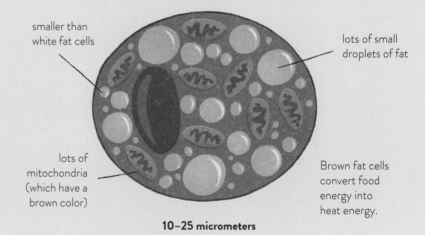

smaller than white fat cells

lots of small droplets of fat

lots of mitochondria (which have a brown color)

Brown fat cells convert food energy into heat energy.

10–25 micrometers

More than a blob

Fat cells are not just blobs full of fat. They store certain vitamins and mop up extra sugar from our blood so it doesn't make us ill. They also make and release some very important chemicals. These include hormones (chemical messengers) that make us feel hungry or full, help control our blood pressure, and activate our immune system when we have an infection.

Inside fat cells, fat is stored as a yellowish liquid that is just like vegetable oil.

BLOOD CELLS

Blood is constantly on the move. As it flows around your body, it delivers food and oxygen to every cell and collects waste ready to be recycled or dumped. The cells floating in your blood help with a host of other jobs too.

Imagine taking all nine pints of blood out of your body and letting it settle, a little like muddy water. (Don't actually try this—you need the blood to stay inside you!) You'd see that blood is mainly plasma (a watery liquid) with three types of blood cells floating in it: red blood cells, white blood cells, and tiny platelets. Each type of cell has a different job to do.

platelets and white blood cells

plasma

red blood cells

The special curved shape of red blood cells helps them soak up as much oxygen as possible.

Red blood cells

Around four in every five of the cells are red blood cells. These are some of the simplest cells in your body—they don't even have a nucleus! Each one is just a bag packed with 300 million molecules of a protein called hemoglobin. You can think of red blood cells as the delivery trucks of your blood, picking up oxygen from your lungs and dropping it off to a different part of your body.

Squash and a squeeze

Blood travels around your body through a network of tunnels— your blood vessels. Some are wide and busy like multilane highways, but some are so narrow that red blood cells must squeeze through in single file! This gives them time to transfer oxygen to or from the cells they are squeezing past.

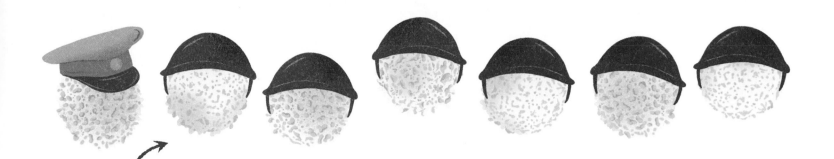

White blood cells

These are part of your body's defense system, known as the immune system. Like a tiny personal army, they patrol your body for invaders, destroying any they find. A lot of them hang out in the blood, so they can quickly get to where they are needed. Discover the different types of white blood cells on pages 40–41.

Plugging holes

Platelets are tiny, disk-shaped pieces of cell. Like red blood cells, they don't have a nucleus. If one of your blood vessels is damaged, blood begins to leak out. Platelets rush to the site of the injury and begin to change shape, forming "tentacles," which stick to the damaged walls and to each other. Together they form a plug, called a clot, which stops the bleeding.

Blood groups

Red blood cells are covered in tiny markers, which tell your white blood cells they belong to your body and shouldn't be destroyed! Everyone has one of four different combinations of markers: A, B, A and B—or O (no markers at all). The combination we have is known as our blood group.

Blood cells don't have long lives. Red blood cells last for about three months, but platelets die after about a week. New blood cells are made in your bone marrow.

One drop of blood contains:

- 15 million platelets
- 500,000 white blood cells
- 250 million red blood cells

An adult makes about a million new platelets every second!

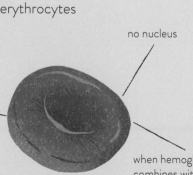

Red blood cells

Scientific name: erythrocytes
Location: blood

no nucleus

"biconcave" shape

packed with hemoglobin proteins

when hemoglobin combines with oxygen, it turns bright red

7 micrometers across

Platelets

Scientific name: thrombocytes
Location: blood

no nucleus

Tiny granules contain chemicals for clotting.

tiny "tentacles" grow from the surface when they are activated; these tentacles only cling to other platelets and to the walls of a damaged blood vessel

just 2–4 micrometers across

BONE CELLS

Bone is a super-strong tissue that's constantly rebuilding itself—even after we stop growing! The construction work is carried out by a trio of incredible cells.

Bone is an amazing tissue that is as strong as steel under pressure, but three times lighter! It forms a skeleton inside our bodies that has three main jobs. It provides places for our muscles to attach so they can pull on our bones to move us around. It protects our soft, squishy organs. Our skeleton also stores important minerals, such as calcium, which is needed by all our body cells. These minerals make up about 60% of the weight of each bone. A quarter of every bone is made up of living cells.

Bone builders

Osteoblasts are cells that work in teams to build new bone. They begin by making a flexible protein called collagen, which they weave together in a matrix. Then the osteoblasts fill the gaps in the matrix with calcium and other minerals, making it strong and rigid.

While you are growing, teams of osteoblasts are hard at work near the end of every long bone in your body, adding new bone every day. These construction sites are known as growth plates.

"Osteo" is the Greek word for "bone."

20

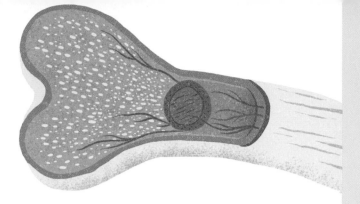

Bone marrow

Bones are compact and hard on the outside, but more like spongy honeycomb near the center. The gaps in this honeycomb are filled with a tissue called bone marrow. New bone cells and blood cells are formed in the marrow.

Bone bosses

Osteocytes are your bones' maintenance crew. They live inside tiny spaces in the bone itself, sending out long "tentacles" to connect to each other. Every cubic millimeter of bone (about the size of a pinhead) contains around 25,000 osteocytes! They sense when bone is damaged or under stress, then tell the osteoclasts and osteoblasts to fix it.

Thanks to your bone cells, your body can repair damaged bones and even adjust the strength of your bones. The more you push and pull on your bones through play and exercise, the stronger they become. The less you use them, the weaker they become.

Demolition workers

Osteoclasts are a squad of demolition cells. They dissolve damaged bone so it can be repaired or made stronger. They also break down bone to release calcium if the rest of your body is running low and needs a boost.

Bone-making cells

Scientific name: osteoblasts
Location: on the surface of bones and in growth plates

cube-shaped or flattened

one nucleus

20 to 50 micrometers

Bone maintenance cells

Scientific name: osteocytes
Location: trapped inside bone tissue

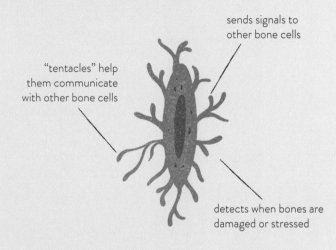

sends signals to other bone cells

"tentacles" help them communicate with other bone cells

detects when bones are damaged or stressed

around 20 micrometers long

Bone demolition cells

Scientific name: osteoclasts
Location: on the surface of bones

large cells

more than one nucleus (because they are made from more than one cell joined together)

An osteoclast gobbles up bone and digests it so the building blocks can be reused.

up to 300 micrometers (a third of a millimeter) across

SKIN CELLS

Your skin is squeezed, stretched, scratched, and scrubbed hundreds of times every day. It might even get bitten, burned, bruised, or blistered. But it always bounces back, thanks to a never-ending supply of skin cells racing to replace each other.

Skin is your body's largest organ. Although it's never more than about 0.15 thick, it covers every part of your body (up to 20 square feet in total) and counts for about a seventh of your total weight!

Building a barrier

The outer layer of our skin—the part we can see—is made up of dead skin cells. They are closely packed and overlap like roof tiles, creating a waterproof barrier against germs, heat, UV light, and toxic chemicals. The strategy of putting dead cells on top is what makes your skin so super successful—a skin cell can't be killed if it is already dead! However, these dead cells are constantly being scratched, scrubbed, or brushed off. You lose up to 40,000 every minute!

Keratin factories

Keratinocytes are skin cells that produce a tough protein called keratin. They begin growing deep down in your skin, getting pushed to the surface as newer cells grow below them. As they grow, they make more and more keratin and beome harder. Eventually they die, just in time to take their place on your skin's surface. It takes 28 days for a keratinocyte to travel from the bottom to the top of the epidermis—meaning you get a brand-new skin every four weeks!

A patch of skin the size of a fingernail has about five million skin cells and at least a thousand sensitive nerve cell endings. It is not as smooth as it looks from a distance!

We shed about a pound of skin every year. In fact, most of the dust in your home is dead skin! This is good news for dust mites who like to munch on it.

Skin has two layers:

1) The top layer (epidermis) is mainly made of keratinocytes, with some melanocytes. It doesn't have any blood vessels.

2) The middle layer (dermis) is made up of a tough but stretchy protein called collagen. This layer has blood vessels to bring food and oxygen; nerve cells to sense touch, heat, pressure, and pain; sweat glands; hair follicles, and oil glands. The oil helps keep the dead skin cells flexible and waterproof. Find out how all these things work together on page 38.

What gives skin its color?

One of the biggest dangers your skin has to cope with is UV radiation in sunlight. Solving this problem is the job of special cells called melanocytes, deep in your epidermis. They make a black pigment called melanin and package it up in granules which they pass on to new skin cells. Melanin protects the skin from UV rays and gives skin its color. The more melanocytes you have, the more melanin your skin can produce.

How thin is skin?

The parts of your skin that get the most wear and tear tend to thicken up. This is why the skin under your feet is thicker than the skin on top.

Skin cells

Scientific name: keratinocytes
Location: outer layer of skin

old, dead cells are flat and rough

rough surface keeps cells locked together

filled with keratin

new cells are boxy and smooth

10–20 micrometers long when flattened

Melanin-making cells

Scientific name: melanocytes
Location: base of the outer layer of skin

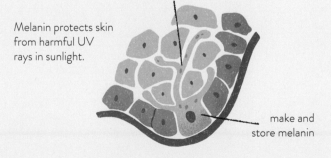

pass granules full of melanin to nearby cells

Melanin protects skin from harmful UV rays in sunlight.

make and store melanin

around 7 micrometers across

LIVER CELLS

Your liver is one of your largest organs. Its multitasking cells carry out hundreds of different jobs every day. Their mission is to supply the rest of your body's cells with the chemicals they need—and to get rid of anything that might be harmful.

An adult's liver weighs up to 3.3 pounds—slightly heavier than their brain! It contains about 20 different types of tissue, but the main one by far is liver tissue, made up of folded sheets of liver cells. These cells are always busy—making, breaking down, and storing hundreds of different chemicals.

Hard workers

A liver cell's job begins when blood full of digested food arrives from the intestines. It filters this blood, removing and breaking down any toxic chemicals that might harm your body. It also sorts through the nutrients you have eaten, storing useful vitamins and minerals, changing food into forms your body cells can use, and storing sugar—or releasing it into your blood if you are running low.

Clean machine

Liver cells also filter out and remove toxic waste made by your own cells, such as ammonia. They are constantly cleaning your blood and making sure it only contains useful stuff.

Sheets of liver cells are surrounded by blood vessels and ducts that carry away bile. These drain into your gallbladder, which stores the bile until your digestive system needs it.

Liver cells
Scientific name: hepatocytes
Location: liver

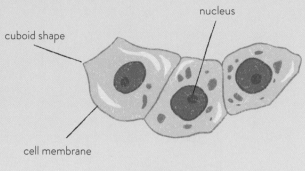

cuboid shape

nucleus

cell membrane

20–30 micrometers

Kupffer cells
Scientific name: liver macrophages
Location: liver

fuzzy coat

hunt and eat old and dying body cells as well as bacteria that have sneaked through from your intestines into your blood

15–20 micrometers

Your liver is also home to special immune system cells known as Kupffer cells. They cling to the walls of blood vessels in your liver, seeking out anything in the incoming blood that shouldn't be there.

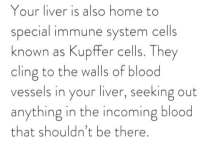

Liver cells produce a greenish liquid called bile, which helps your body digest fats. Your liver makes up to two pints of bile every day!

Gatekeepers
If Kupffer cells find a worn-out and dying cell, a germ or anything else suspicious, they gobble it up! They are your liver's sniffer dogs.

SEX CELLS

Most cells made by our bodies have a full set of instructions for building a human. Sex cells are different—they have only half the instructions.

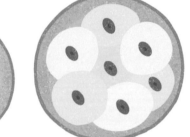
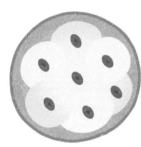

Our bodies begin making mature sex cells when we go through puberty. Male and female bodies each make a different type of sex cell. Male bodies make sperm cells. Female bodies make egg cells. When a sperm cell meets with an egg cell, the instructions carried by each one combine to make a cell with a complete instruction book for making a human! This cell may begin to develop into a new human.

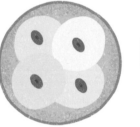

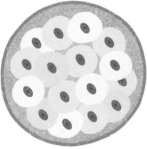

What happens after a sperm cell meets an egg cell?

1) A sperm cell and an egg cell join to form a fertilized cell, or zygote. The zygote makes a copy of itself. Each cell gets a copy of the instruction book.

2) Next, each of these cells splits into two, making four cells. Then splits again, making eight cells, and so on.

3) After seven days, the single zygote has become a ball of cells about as big as a pinhead.

4) At the center is a cluster of 30 very special cells, called stem cells. These cells have the power to become any of the 200 different types of human cells!

5) The stem cells continue dividing. After about 14 days, they begin to specialize. Some will become intestine or lung cells. Some will become bone, blood, or heart cells.

6) By making copies of themselves, this tiny bundle of cells can develop into a new baby, made up of trillions of cells. This takes around 40 weeks from start to finish.

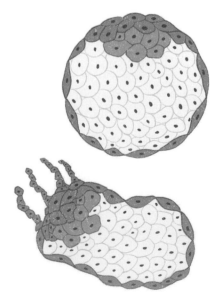

Sperm

Sperm cells are made in a male's testes, starting around the time of puberty. Thousands of new sperm are made every day. Each sperm has a long tail, which helps it swim and look for an egg cell.

Eggs

After puberty, female ovaries release one egg cell every month. The egg cells are huge compared to sperm cells. They contain lots of nutrients, which will be used if the cell becomes fertilized and begins to develop into a new human.

Egg cells are surrounded by smaller cells from the ovary. They supply the egg cell with nutrients.

Egg cell

Scientific name: ovum
Location: formed in female ovaries

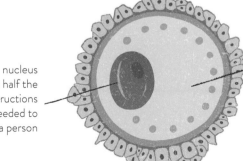

nucleus with half the instructions needed to make a person

lots of nutrients in cytoplasm

120 micrometers, often visible without a microscope

Sperm cell

Scientific name: spermatozoon
Location: formed in male testes

long tail for swimming

head with half the instructions needed to make a person

mitochondrion breaks down fuel to release energy for swimming

50 micrometers long

Chapter 3

FROM CELLS TO SYSTEMS

Your body is a vast community, where 30 trillion cells live closely together. Like any metropolis, it relies on well-organized systems to keep it running smoothly.

This chapter takes a closer look at some of the main systems that make up your body. They include food processing, transportation, and waste disposal systems, as well as a system of defenses to keep out dangerous invaders and a security force to deal with any that sneak in. Your body also has a control center that makes decisions and a communications network to pass these messages on.

Your **nervous system** and **brain** monitor the world around you and tell your body how to respond.

Your **skeletomuscular system** moves you around so you can do the things you need to survive.

Your **immune system** (lymphatic system) deals with harmful invaders—and any of your own cells that go rogue.

Your **digestive system** breaks food down into particles small enough to be used by cells.

Don't ever change

Your body systems are all linked, and they all depend on each other. When a cell carries out a certain job within your digestive system or your respiratory system, it is not only helping the other cells in that system. It is helping every other cell in your body. As different as they are, most of your body systems have the same overall task: to keep things the same!

Your **respiratory system** collects the oxygen your cells need to unlock the energy in food, and it gets rid of the carbon dioxide they produce as they do it.

Your **reproductive system** gets your body ready to pass on its genetic information (your cells may not be immortal, but your genes try to be!).

Your **cardiovascular system** makes sure all your cells have a constant supply of food and oxygen.

Your **excretory system** (urinary system) gets rid of toxic waste.

Your cells are picky. They like . . .

- a toasty temperature of 98.6°F
- just the right amount of water
- a constant supply of food
- a constant supply of oxygen
- someone to clean up after them.

If conditions change, your cells complain! Your body systems jump into action to put it right, keeping conditions ideal for each of your 30 trillion cells to do their best work!

DIGESTIVE SYSTEM

Each of your 30 trillion cells needs to feed. Getting hold of this food is the job of your digestive system—a long tube that begins at the mouth and ends at the bottom!

Laid out from end to end, your digestive system would be around 30 feet long (don't check this at home as it's hard to fold everything back into the right place!). As food travels through this long tube, it's broken down into pieces tiny enough to pass into your cells—pieces around 10 million times smaller than a pea. It's a bit like breaking Mount Everest down into grains of sand! Your digestive system is lined with different types of cells that each play a role in this mountainous task.

Muscle cells

Food doesn't just drop down your esophagus. Smooth muscle cells in its walls work together to squeeze the food toward your stomach. They would get the job done even if you were standing on your head.

Lining cells

The "skin" lining your digestive system is softer and slimier than the skin outside your body. Special goblet cells constantly release mucus to protect the lining cells from being scratched by your food or digested themselves. Even so, these cells wear away quickly as you bite, chew, and swallow, and so they are replaced every four to five days.

Acid-squirting cells

Your stomach lining has at least four types of cells that squirt out different chemicals, including enzymes to break down proteins and fats, chemical messengers to tell your body when your stomach is full and strong acid to kill any germs that hitched a ride on your meal.

Tiny helpers

An army of nonhuman cells lives in your intestines, helping your digestive system break down food. These microbes (dead and alive) make up at least a third of your poop whenever you go to the bathroom!

Super soaker cells

Carbohydrates, proteins, fats, vitamins, and minerals are all broken down into particles tiny enough to be soaked up by the "hairy" cells lining your small intestine. They pass through these cells and into your blood. Their next stop will be your liver.

Butterfly cells

The cells lining your digestive system include nerve cells that send your brain information about digestion. When we feel nervous or worried about something, our brains often divert blood away from our stomach to get our muscles ready for action. The digestive system nerve cells "complain" about this, creating "butterflies" in our stomach!

Stomach lining cells

Scientific name: parietal cells
Location: stomach lining

secrete gastric acid

These cells can only live for three days in this dangerous, acidic environment.

around 20 micrometers

Intestine lining cells

Scientific name: enterocytes
Location: intestine lining

surface of the cell is folded into tiny "fingers" to give more space for soaking up food

column-shaped

cytoplasm

food is carried right though these lining cells and out the other side, ready to enter a blood vessel

Each of the fingers on top is just one micrometre high.

Goblet cells

Scientific name: mucosal epithelial cell
Location: in the walls of the digestive system

shaped like an old-fashioned cup, or goblet

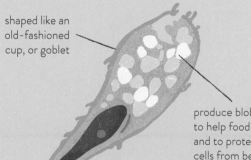

produce blobs of mucus to help food pass through and to protect the lining cells from being digested themselves

11 micrometers across

RESPIRATORY SYSTEM

Food is fuel for your body's cells. Like all fuel, it won't burn without oxygen. Your respiratory system gets hold of this oxygen with the help of a snot escalator!

Take a deep breath and you can feel air traveling through your respiratory system . . . in through your nostrils and mouth, down your trachea (windpipe), forking into two large tubes called bronchi, then branching into smaller and smaller tubes and inflating 300 million tiny, stretchy sacs called alveoli.

Stretchy sacs

The walls of each alveolus are just one cell thick! As the alveoli fill with air, oxygen easily passes through this layer of cells and into blood vessels on the other side—a journey of just one thousandth of a millimeter. Carbon dioxide passes in the opposite direction and then leaves your body as you breathe out.

Your body can't store oxygen, so your respiratory system works 24/7. Most people can only hold their breath for 30 to 90 seconds before their cells start protesting.

The walls of the alveoli are made up of two main types of cells. The first are like simple, flat "bricks" in the wall. The second type are bigger and produce a soapy substance that stops the walls of the alveoli from sticking together like a damp sock when you breathe out.

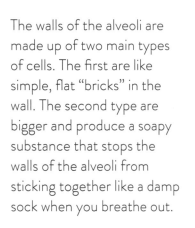

carbon dioxide — — oxygen

alveolus

blood vessel

Out there air

The respiratory system is constantly bringing the outside world into your body—and this air is rarely pure. In fact, it's often carrying an invisible but disgusting mix of germs, pollen, dust, and tiny particles of pollution. How does your respiratory system deal with this? It builds a snot escalator!

The cells lining the tubes leading into your lungs are very different from those lining the alveoli themselves. Most are covered in tiny hairs. There are also lots of goblet cells, which spew out blobs of sticky mucus. The mucus traps particles, then the hairs push this snotty sludge up out of your lungs and into your throat, where it gets coughed out of your body or swallowed. (Your stomach acid takes care of the rest!)

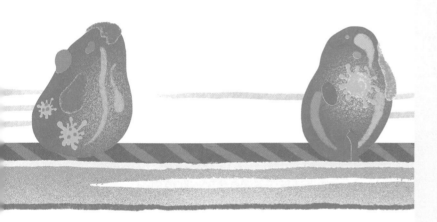

If the linings of every alveolus in your body were laid out like a patchwork quilt, they would cover an area about the size of a tennis court.

Simple lining cells

Scientific name: type I pneumocytes
Location: lining the alveoli in your lungs

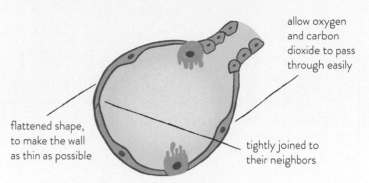

allow oxygen and carbon dioxide to pass through easily

flattened shape, to make the wall as thin as possible

tightly joined to their neighbors

Can be more than 2,000 micrometers (2 millimeters) long, but just a tenth of a micrometre thick!

Surfactant-secreting cell

Scientific name: type II pneumocytes
Location: lining the alveoli in your lungs

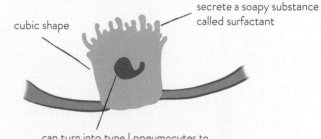

cubic shape

secrete a soapy substance called surfactant

can turn into type I pneumocytes to replace any that get damaged

just 9 micrometers across

Hairy lining cells

Scientific name: ciliated epithelial cells
Location: the tubes that lead into your lungs

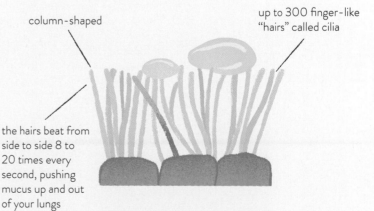

column-shaped

up to 300 finger-like "hairs" called cilia

the hairs beat from side to side 8 to 20 times every second, pushing mucus up and out of your lungs

Cilia are around 5 micrometers long but just a fifth of a micrometre thick.

33

CARDIOVASCULAR SYSTEM

Once food and oxygen have been gathered, they must be transported to every cell in your body. This is the job of the cardiovascular system.

Your blood is the tissue that carries food and oxygen around your body. Your heart is the organ that keeps it moving, through a vast network of blood vessels. Together these things make up your cardiovascular (or circulatory) system.

As well as making sure every cell has the energy and nutrients it needs to do its job, the circulatory system collects waste produced by cells and takes it to where it can be recycled or removed from your body.

Blood vessels form two separate loops in your body. The smallest loop takes blood from your heart to your lungs, where it dumps carbon dioxide and picks up oxygen, then right back to your heart again. From here, the blood is sent off on a much longer loop, through a network of blood vessels that takes in every part of your body from the skin on your scalp to the tips of your toes.

artery

End to end, your blood vessels would wrap more than four times around Earth!

Superhighways

The network begins with large arteries, bulging with the pressure of all the blood being pushed through them. These branch off into smaller vessels and eventually into very narrow tubes called capillaries.

As they take this scenic route, red blood cells give up their oxygen to the cells surrounding the capillaries and pick up carbon dioxide in return. No cell in your body is far from a capillary—you can even spot them branching through the whites of your eyes!

Main roads

Capillaries join again to form larger vessels known as veins, which lead back to the heart. Blood arrives at the heart with a heavy load of carbon dioxide, ready to start the entire journey again.

Capillary lining cells

Scientific name: capillary endothelial cells
Location: the walls of your capillaries

flattened, to make the walls as thin as possible

even the nucleus is flattened

curved shape

tightly joined to neighbouring cells to make sure capillaries don't leak

membrane chooses what passes in and out of the cell

50–70 micrometers long, but just 0.1 –10 micrometers thick

singular vein

To the lungs -->

O_2

O_2 O_2

CO_2

capillaries

Country roads

Capillaries are narrower than the hairs on your head, and their walls are just one cell thick to help oxygen and nutrients pass through easily. These cells don't just let anything in and out of your blood. They carefully select which molecules can pass through.

Cellular respiration

When we talk about respiration, we often think about breathing. But respiration is also a chemical reaction happening in every cell of your body. Sugar reacts with oxygen to produce carbon dioxide and water. This also releases energy in a form that the cell can use. Carbon dioxide would poison your cells if it built up, so it is passed to your blood to take back to your lungs, where it can be breathed out. The water (about 10 fluid ounces or a large glassful every day) is reused by your body.

35

SKELETOMUSCULAR SYSTEM

With a body 30 trillion times bigger than an amoeba, it's no wonder you need a whole system dedicated to holding it up and hauling you around.

Your skeletomuscular system is really two systems that work very closely together. Your skeletal system is made up of bones that support your body and protect your squishiest organs. Your muscular system pulls on these bones to move them around.

Each muscle in your body is attached to bones on different sides of a joint. This turns the bones into levers. Muscles pull on bones by making themselves shorter. Muscles can relax and get longer again, but they can't push on a bone. So they always work in pairs: your biceps muscle contracts to bend your arm, and your triceps muscle contracts to open it up again.

From cells to fibers

Skeletal muscles look stripey under a microscope. This is a clue to how muscle cells build muscle tissue. Skeletal muscles are made of bundles of fibers, which themselves are bundles of very long cells. When the muscle is relaxed, the fibers overlap only slightly. When the muscle gets an electrical signal from the nervous system, the cells release chemicals that make the fibers slide together and overlap more. This makes the muscle shorter. As it gets shorter, it tugs on the bones it is attached to.

Muscle tissue contains lots of capillaries to supply muscle cells with oxygen and fuel. This gives muscles their bright pink color.

The 42 muscles in your face help you show other people exactly how you are feeling!

Skeletal muscle cells

Scientific name: myocytes
Location: your skeletal muscles

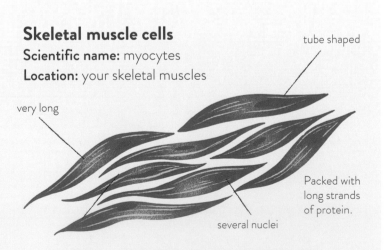

tube shaped

very long

Packed with long strands of protein.

several nuclei

Usually 0.75–1 inch long, but can be up to 12 inches long.

In total, you have about 640 different skeletal muscles that you can control just by thinking about moving them.

cartilage

Multitasking muscles

Muscles are hard at work even when you're still. Tiny sensors in your muscles constantly send your brain information about muscle length and tension, and your brain constantly suggests tiny adjustments that hold your body where you want it to be. Muscle contractions also produce most of the heat energy that keeps your body warm at 98.6°F.

Cartilage

Cartilage is a tough, slippery tissue that forms over the ends of bones where they meet at joints. It also forms flexible parts of your skeleton, such as your outer ears. Cartilage is made by cells called chondrocytes.

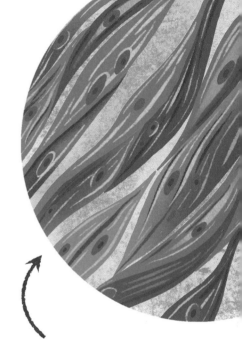

The tubes of your digestive and respiratory systems are surrounded by a different type of muscle, known as smooth muscle. It contracts and relaxes automatically, without you needing to think about it.

INTEGUMENTARY SYSTEM

Skin is the barrier between your body's 30 trillion cells and the rest of the world. It's a superhero with several sidekicks, including hair, nails, oil, and sweat. Together, these fab five make up your integumentary system!
(Yes, they could do with a catchier name.)

Your integumentary system is mainly made of dead cells and slightly gross secretions. Together they protect the living cells inside from a host of outside threats, including invading germs, toxic chemicals, allergens, extreme temperatures, and bumps and scratches. They also stop water escaping from your body in an uncontrolled way. Your body takes water very seriously.

These are the villains to the superheroes of the IG system!

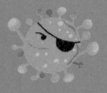    

invading germs   **toxic chemicals**   **allergens**   **dangerous rays**   **bumps and scratches**   **extreme temperatures**

All-arounders
Skin cells are great at regenerating and repairing themselves. Alongside their protective role, they carry out a host of freelance jobs, including making vitamin D and detecting pressure, pain, and temperature changes.

Cooling system
Skin helps keep our body temperature as close as possible to 98.6°F. If we get too warm, capillaries in our skin widen and let blood rush to the surface, where they lose heat to the air. Glands in our skin release sweat, which uses our body heat to evaporate, speeding up the cooling process. If we get too cool, the capillaries in our skin narrow.

Hairs on your head grow around 0.01 inches every day. Fingernails grow more slowly—just 0.02 inches a week.

bead of sweat

sweat duct

Hair and nails

Just like skin, our hairs and fingernails are made of dead cells filled with keratin. Extra cells are added to the base of a hair or a nail all the time, pushing the cells above upward so the hair or nail grows. Nails are like built-in armor, protecting our fingers and toes from damage.

Hair colors

Our hair gets its color in the same way that our skin does. Cells called melanocytes pass tiny granules into newly formed hair cells. The granules contain a pigment called melanin. There are two types of melanin, and the mixture of types, as well as the amount that is passed on and how spread out it becomes, gives each strand of hair its unique color. As people get older, their melanocytes become less active and stop passing on as much melanin. The cells—and eventually the entire strand—becomes white or gray.

Hairs embedded in our skin stand on end, trapping a layer of warm air next to our skin.

Melanin-making cells

Scientific name: melanocytes
Location: base of the outer layer of skin

make and store melanin

pass granules full of melanin to nearby cells

Melanin protects skin from harmful UV rays in sunlight.

the white part at the base of each hair hasn't yet been injected with melanin by the melanocytes

up to 20 micrometers long

Not so secret secretions

Skin also has glands that produce sweat, oily sebum and earwax. Sweat helps control our body temperature and gives us a unique smell. Sebum helps keep skin flexible and waterproof. Cerumen (the scientific name for earwax) is a mix of sweat, sebum, and dead skin cells. Its job is to trap dirt, germs, and anything else that might damage your ear. It also keeps the entrance to your ear dry so microbes are less likely to set up camp.

IMMUNE SYSTEM

If microbes do make it past your snotty, sweaty, earwax-y defenses, all is not lost. Your immune system is your personal army, ready to track down and eliminate anything that shouldn't be there.

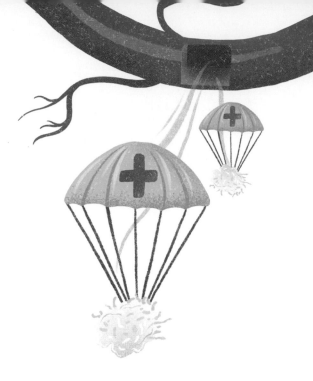

It's hard to draw the immune system because it's everywhere! It's an army of different cells, each focusing on a certain job. It works closely with the lymphatic system, which is a network of tiny vessels and little bean-shaped lumps called lymph nodes. Organs such as your thymus, spleen, and tonsils are part of this system, too.

Immune cells known as white blood cells start life in your bone marrow, then travel to your thymus gland or to a lymph node to finish developing. Here they become specialized to help with two different kinds of defense.

"Just in case" defense

When your body senses any kind of damage or invasion, white blood cells called neutrophils and monocytes rush to the site. The capillary walls in that area become leaky to let them through, like traffic pulling over to let emergency vehicles past. Once they are in the damaged tissue, they go around gobbling up anything that looks suspicious. This might be germs, toxins, or even your own cells that have been invaded by viruses or damaged by sunburn.

Each monocyte can eat up to 100 enemy cells before it dies. All that leaking fluid and all those dead, germ-filled white blood cells might make the area swollen and sore.

Targeted defense

Your immune system can also train itself to learn the weaknesses of specific enemies and defeat them quicker next time they appear. This involves a separate set of white blood cells, known as lymphocytes. After a monocyte destroys an enemy cell, it tears off certain parts—known as antigens—and presents them to the lymphocytes. This reprograms the lymphocytes to tag that kind of antigen with tiny "flags" called antibodies. The flags makes the enemy cells easier for monocytes to recognize.

Germ memory

The first time a germ gets into your body, it takes your lymphocytes a few days to learn how to make the right antibodies. But a few of these reprogrammed lymphocytes stay in your body even after an infection. Next time that germ gets into your body, they spring into action right away, helping your immune system destroy the germ before it can multiply and make you ill. You have become immune to that germ.

In between cells

Lymph fluid collects in the spaces between your body cells and drains into the lymphatic system. At certain points, the lymph fluid drains into your blood, carrying its army of white blood cells with it.

All-arounders

Scientific name: neutrophil
Location: your blood and lymph fluid

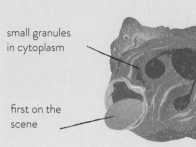

nucleus with different lobes

small granules in cytoplasm

Chase germs and destroy them.

Work faster than macrophages but can't eat as much.

first on the scene

9–15 micrometers

Big eaters

Scientific name: monocytes
Location: your blood, lymph and body tissues

huge, round nucleus

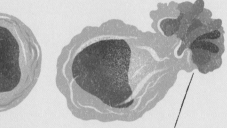

Can leave your blood and move into a body tissue, where it becomes a macrophage ('big eater').

chase, engulf and destroy germs

15–18 micrometers

Adaptive white blood cells

Scientific name: lymphocytes
Location: your blood and lymph fluid

T cells attack specific enemy cells

B cells make antibodies that cling to specific enemy cells

huge, round nucleus

7–15 micrometers

EXCRETORY SYSTEM

Thirty trillion cells hard at work produce a LOT of waste. Your cells get rid of this waste by dumping it into your blood. Then your excretory system removes it from your body . . . by making urine!

Anything can be toxic for cells if there is too much of it, even water. So your excretory system also adjusts the amount of water in your body. It does this by changing how much water is turned into urine. The urinary system includes your kidneys, bladder, and the tubes that connect them. It also includes your urethra —a tube that carries urine out of your body.

Filtration system
Urine is just water with waste chemicals dissolved in it. To make it, your kidneys constantly filter your blood. Each kidney is made up of more than a million identical parts called nephrons.

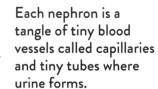

Each nephron is a tangle of tiny blood vessels called capillaries and tiny tubes where urine forms.

Ur-ine shape
Urine collects at the center of each kidney before draining into your bladder. The cells that line your bladder have a special shape, which means the lining can be **stretched** a huge amount without tearing. There are also nerve cells, which signal to your brain when you need to go to the bathroom.

Leftovers

The liquid left behind is urine. It is mainly water and usually contains salts, acids, and lots of urea (one of the main waste products produced by your body cells). It may also contain sugar, proteins, vitamins that dissolve in water, and cells worn away from the lining of your excretory system. Every day your body gets rid of about 1.75 ounces of stuff dissolved in your pee!

Bladder lining cells

Scientific name: transitional epithelial cells
Location: the wall of your bladder, kidneys, and the tubes that join them

tightly packed so nothing leaks out

soft and round at the top, so they can stretch

covered in mucus to protect themselves from the slightly acidic urine

Around 12 micrometers, but can stretch a lot bigger.

Every blood cell in your body passes through one of your kidneys every four minutes!

Nephrons

As blood is squeezed through a nephron, almost EVERYTHING in it—water, salts, nutrients, waste—is forced out of the blood and into the tiny tubes. Only red and white blood cells and chunky molecules like proteins are left behind. Bit by bit, the cells that line your kidneys let only the useful things that your body needs back into the blood, in exactly the amounts that your body needs.

Why is urine yellow?

People once believed that the yellow color was from gold and spent lots of time trying to collect the precious metal from their pee . . . with disappointing results! The color actually comes from a chemical that is made when your liver breaks down old blood cells.

NERVOUS SYSTEM

Your nervous system coordinates the work of 30 trillion cells, helping them collect information, communicate, and cooperate. Every second it sends millions of electrical signals traveling around your body as fast as a speeding train.

Your nervous system has three main parts:

- sensory organs monitor what is happening inside and outside your body
- a brain ponders this information and decides what to do
- a huge network of nerves sends signals to organs, tissues, and cells, telling them to take action.

All these parts are made up of different kinds of nerve cells, known as neurons. Most of your body's neurons are gathered in your brain, but millions more form a network all around your body.

Move your finger

A "nerve" is a bundle of nerve cell axons, linking different places in your body. Some nerves carry signals to your brain. Others carry signals from your brain to parts of your body that take action, such as muscles. But most nerves have cells carrying messages in both directions.

Processing power

Neurons are very different from other types of cells. They form long "fingers" called dendrites and axons, which reach out and form connections with many other cells. These connections mean a single nerve cell can communicate almost instantly with tens of thousands of others.

Nerve cells

Scientific name: neurons
Location: your entire body

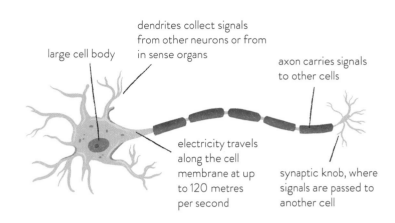

dendrites collect signals from other neurons or from in sense organs

large cell body

axon carries signals to other cells

electricity travels along the cell membrane at up to 120 metres per second

synaptic knob, where signals are passed to another cell

The largest nerve cells have processes that reach from the bottom of your spine to the tips of your toes!

Schwann cell

Scientific name: neurolemmocytes
Location: wrapped around nerves outside your brain and spinal cord

makes fatty myelin, which doesn't conduct electricity well

neuron

grows around the axon of a neuron, like the coating on an electrical wire

helps electrical signals travel faster through the axon, without leaking or getting weaker

up to 400 micrometers (0.4 millimeters) long

Neurons can also "remember" the pathways that messages have taken through this tangled network in the past, speeding up communication even more.

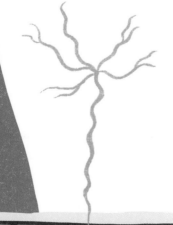

Sending signals

When a nerve cell gets excited by something, chemical changes produce a tiny pulse of electricity that travels along the cell membrane like a wave. When the electrical signal reaches the end of the axon, it may (if it is strong enough) trigger chemical changes in the next nerve cell, which sets up a new electrical signal. All this happens in about a thousandth of a second! Your brain decodes these signals by looking at which nerve cells they are coming from and how often they are being sent. Let's have a look at how this works in your eyes . . .

Eye see you

Your eyes gather more information about the world than all your other senses combined! This information is in the form of light energy bouncing off the objects all around you. Your eye focuses incoming light on the lining of the back of your eye. This lining—called the retina—is packed with millions of special cells that get excited when light hits them. There are two types: rods and cones.

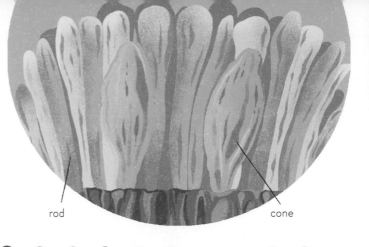

rod

cone

Cones

There are around seven million cone cells in each retina. Cone cells each get excited by one color of light—either red, blue, or green. Your brain compares the signals from different cone cells to figure out what color you're seeing. For example, purple light will trigger red and blue cones.

CONE CELLS aren't triggered by dim light, so we can't see colors well in the dark. But we can still see thanks to rod cells.

Cone cells

Scientific name: cone photoreceptors
Location: the back of your eyes

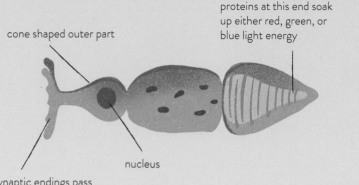

cone shaped outer part

proteins at this end soak up either red, green, or blue light energy

nucleus

synaptic endings pass signals on to nerve cells

up to 50 micrometers long but just 1–4 micrometers across

Rod cells

Scientific name: rod photoreceptors
Location: the back of your eyes

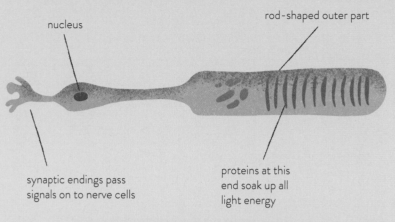

nucleus

rod-shaped outer part

synaptic endings pass signals on to nerve cells

proteins at this end soak up all light energy

100 micrometers long but just 2 micrometers across

Are you in control?

Some parts of your nervous system are under conscious control. For example, you can choose where to look by getting your brain to send signals to the muscles that swivel your eyes. Other nervous signals are sent automatically. For example, your brain monitors the amount of light energy hitting your retinas. If the light is very bright, it sends signals to muscles that make your pupils smaller to protect the sensitive rod and cone cells.

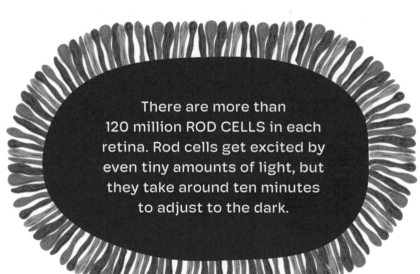

There are more than 120 million ROD CELLS in each retina. Rod cells get excited by even tiny amounts of light, but they take around ten minutes to adjust to the dark.

Optic nerve

The electrical signals that begin in your cone and rod cells are passed on to the optic nerve—an information superhighway made up of around a million nerve cells! These cells carry the signals directly to your brain, which decodes them to create images of the world.

Your brain can sometimes get mixed up—if you stare at one color for a long time, the cone cells for that color get tired and stop working. Test this by staring at the red T-shirt for 20 seconds. Then move your eyes and stare at the white T-shirt. For a few moments, only your other cone cells are triggered by the light bouncing off the white paper, so your brain "sees" an afterimage of a different color!

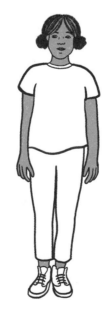

ENDOCRINE SYSTEM

Your nervous system is your body's high-speed broadband service, letting different tissues, organs, and systems send ultrafast messages. Your endocrine system is snail mail in comparison, but its chemical messages help control the rate at which you grow, when you get sleepy, and even how hungry, happy, scared, or worried you feel.

The chemical messages produced by your endocrine system are known as hormones. There are more than 50 different kinds. They are made and released by cells and tissues scattered all around your body, from the pituitary gland in your brain to the thyroid gland in your neck to certain cells in your pancreas.

Traveling keys

Hormones are released into your blood so your cardiovascular system can carry them around your entire body. However, hormones are not spam email. Each hormone only has the power to activate certain cells in your body. They are messages that can only get through doors in those target cells.

pancreas

thyroid gland

adrenal gland

ovaries (female)

When hormones find a target cell they might:
- tell it to start work
- tell it to store or release a certain substance
- tell it to grow and make copies of itself.

Unlocking doors

Each cell already knows what kind of cell it is; hormones just tell it how quickly to do its jobs, if at all. For example, your pancreas has cells that make hormones called insulin and glucagon. Insulin tells target cells to take in and store sugar. Glucagon does the opposite. Together, these hormones keep the amount of sugar in your blood steady. These hormone-producing cells are found in little "islands" in your pancreas.

Insulin binds with receptors on the outside of target cells, like a key fitting a lock. This opens tiny doors that let molecules of sugar enter the cell.

these cells make digestive enzymes

cluster of alpha and beta cells, which control blood sugar levels

there are about a million of these clusters in your pancreas

Who tells endocrine cells what to do?

Two glands in your brain are the postmasters of the endocrine system. They produce hormones that target and activate cells in other parts of your endocrine system, telling them when it's time to produce and release their own hormones. Some endocrine cells are also triggered by chemicals that aren't hormones. For example, pancreas cells begin producing insulin when they detect extra sugar in your blood after a meal.

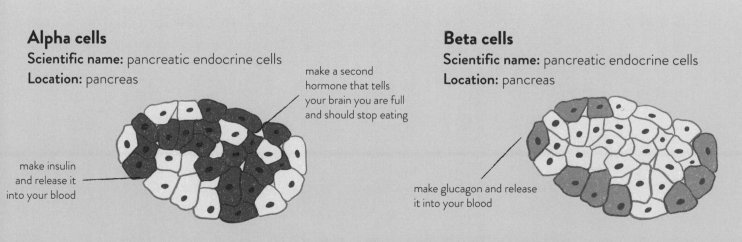

Alpha cells
Scientific name: pancreatic endocrine cells
Location: pancreas

make insulin and release it into your blood

make a second hormone that tells your brain you are full and should stop eating

Beta cells
Scientific name: pancreatic endocrine cells
Location: pancreas

make glucagon and release it into your blood

Each islet is up to a tenth of a millimeter wide and contains around 2,000 cells.

WHERE DO CELLS COME FROM?

Each of us begins life as a single cell. Over time, we grow into a walking, talking, thinking colony of at least 30 trillion cells! Where do they all come from? And how do they know which types of cells they are supposed to be?

The short answer is that cells come from other cells. A new cell is made when an existing cell splits in two, making a copy of itself. This is happening all around your body, right now. Cells clone themselves to replace old or damaged cells and to repair tissues. If enough cells are actively dividing, you grow too!

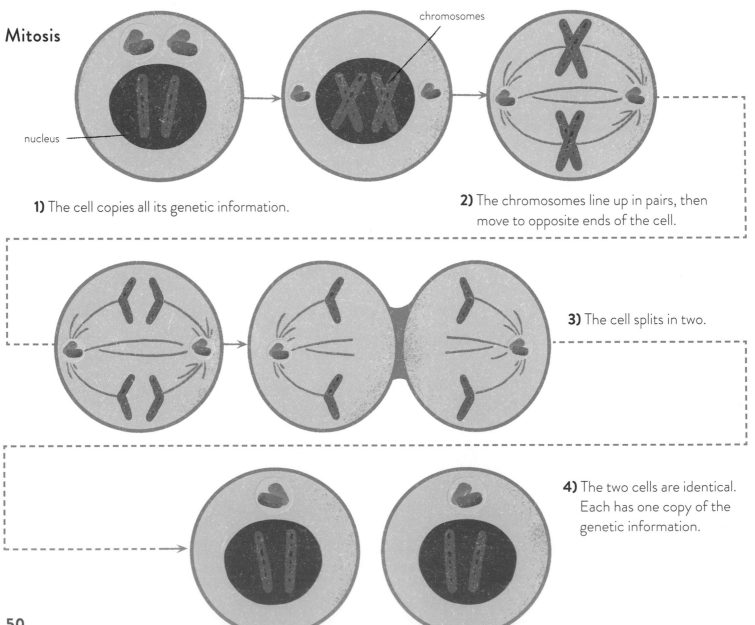

Mitosis

chromosomes

nucleus

1) The cell copies all its genetic information.

2) The chromosomes line up in pairs, then move to opposite ends of the cell.

3) The cell splits in two.

4) The two cells are identical. Each has one copy of the genetic information.

If cells come from cells, where did the first cell come from?

The truth is that no one knows. Scientists have figured out that the first life on Earth appeared sometime between 3.7 and 4.5 billion years ago. There is also evidence that those first cells were fairly simple. They did not have the fancy organelles that your cells have. They may have been more like today's bacteria.

Either way, we know that the very first cell was the ancestor of ALL living things on Earth, including you! This means we can learn a lot about our own cells by studying the cells of other living things.

Adult stem cells

Scientific name: mesenchymal stem cells
Location: certain tissues, such as bone marrow and skin

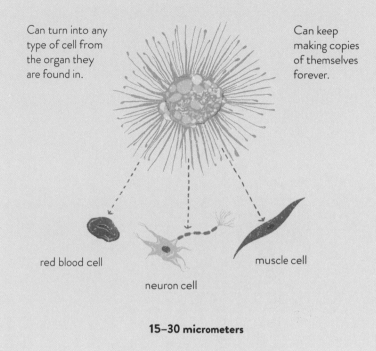

Can turn into any type of cell from the organ they are found in.

Can keep making copies of themselves forever.

red blood cell

neuron cell

muscle cell

15–30 micrometers

How do cells know which type of cell to become?

The process begins with stem cells. These special cells don't have a fixed type such as "skin cell" or "brain cell." They have options! Each stem cell can keep dividing to make more stem cells. Or it can turn itself into a certain type of cell. The decision it makes depends on:

• clues from nearby cells
• chemical messages released by more distant cells
• other factors, such as how much food is available.

Your body's cells aren't on autopilot. They are constantly getting clues from other cells, near and far. They are communicating, cooperating, and learning how to work together to build the best possible version of you!

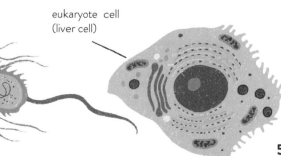

eukaryote cell
(liver cell)

prokaryote cell
(bacterium)

WHEN CELLS GO WRONG

Most of the time our 30 trillion cells work so well that we don't even think about them. If tissues get damaged or worn, they are good at repairing or replacing themselves. But certain illnesses are caused by cells not doing what they are supposed to do.

Sometimes certain cells have missing or changed instructions, which means they can't make a certain protein needed for the cells to work properly. For example, sickle cell anemia is caused by a change in the instructions that tell cells how to make the protein that carries oxygen around our bodies.

Someone's changed the locks

Sometimes certain cells gradually stop working. Some people develop an illness called type 2 diabetes when their cells stop responding to insulin (*see page 49*). It's as if the locks have been changed and the insulin can't pass on its message to cells anymore.

red blood cell

Damaged cells

Sometimes cells are damaged by an illness or accident and cannot be fully repaired or replaced. For example, the nerve cells in your brain and spine make many connections as you grow and develop, and some are impossible to replicate if they get damaged.

sickle cell

coronavirus

Viruses

Sometimes our cells get hijacked by a virus, which tricks the cell into making lots of new copies of the virus. They harm our cells when they burst out and infect new cells.

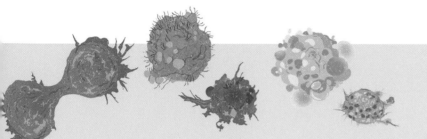

virus particles

human cell

Cancer cell

Scientific name: depends on which part of the body they come from—for example, carcinomas are cancers that begin as epithelial cells such as skin cells.

Location: a cell can begin growing out of control almost anywhere in the body; the type of cell it is determines what kind of cancer it is and how it is treated, even if it moves to a different part of the body.

Abnormal cells

Sometimes a cell starts to grow out of control. It makes copies of itself without being told to. It ignores signals telling it to stop dividing. The copies also behave like this. They might travel into nearby tissues or even to other parts of the body and begin growing in the wrong place. This is known as cancer. Scientists and doctors have learned a lot about how cancers begin and how to help our bodies get rid of these abnormal cells if they start to grow.

Lifesaving cells

Tiny changes to tiny cells can cause big problems. Luckily, your immune system is very good at tracking down cells that have gone wrong and eliminating them. Medicines can help us feel better while this happens or even give our immune systems a helping hand. Scientists are also finding ways to use stem cells to help replace cells that have missing or changed instructions. In the future, these new kinds of treatments could save millions of lives.

53

WHY DON'T CELLS LIVE FOREVER?

If cells can make new cells, why aren't we immortal? We can understand why people grow old by looking closely at what happens to cells over time.

Even when we stop growing, our bodies are constantly making new cells to replace cells that have become worn or damaged. Most cells can only divide between 40 to 60 times before they stop working properly, so we rely on special cells called stem cells, which never stop being able to make copies of themselves.

Over time even stem cells get worn out. They become less good at making copies of themselves, which means our bodies become less good at replacing damaged or worn-out cells. Gradually tissues and organs stop working as well as they once did.

Ear, ear

We are born with about 15,000 hair cells in each ear. Each cell is topped with a bundle of very sensitive hairs, which vibrate when sounds reach our ears. The cells detect these vibrations and change them into nerve signals that are sent to our brain. Loud sounds can damage the tiny hairs—like a hurricane damages a forest—and they can't be replaced or repaired. This is why loud sounds can lead to hearing loss.

Healthy hair cell in your inner ear

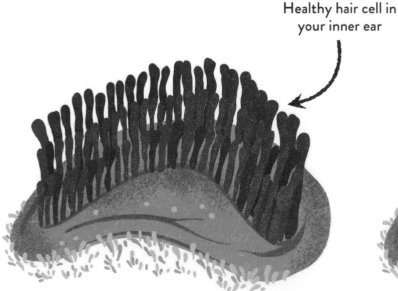

Hair cell after a loud sound

As people become older:
- Some cells get less good at taking in nutrients and making proteins. This can change the appearance of tissues such as skin.
- Some cells stop repairing and replacing tissues at the same rate, which is why bones become more fragile.
- Some cells get less good at clearing away waste. This can affect how quickly brain and nerve cells pass on messages.
- Some cells die and cannot be replaced. As we age, the number of hair cells in our ears naturally falls. Our body can't make new ones, so we can't hear the same range of sounds.

Telomeres

Every time a cell makes a copy of itself, it loses a tiny piece of DNA from the end of each chromosome. At first, this doesn't make a difference because our chromosomes are "padded" with extra DNA that isn't needed. But once these ends, called telomeres, have become too short, a cell dies.

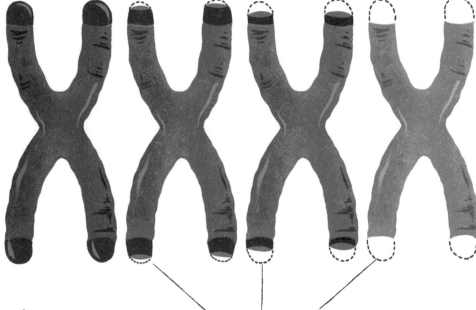

shortening telemeres

Natural process

Although aging and dying are natural parts of a human life, we can help keep our cells healthy by eating and drinking healthily and exercising regularly. Many of our body systems make extra cells only if they are needed, so when it comes to healthy muscles, bones, heart, lungs, and even brain it's a case of "use it or lose it." You can also protect the most fragile cells in your body—for example, by not listening to loud music through headphones.

Chapter 5

30 TRILLION MORE

Your 30 trillion cells are not alone in the world. Your body is also home to at least 30 trillion cells that are not human!

Your body is home to trillions of tiny living creatures, known as microbes. There are many different kinds, but they are all made up of just one cell. Each of these single-celled creatures does all the things needed to stay alive: growing, moving, feeding, getting rid of waste and reproducing. Their habitat just happens to be your body!

Our tiny microbe passengers were first discovered around 350 years ago, when a scientist scrapped some "scurf" off his teeth and peered at it under a microscope. He was amazed to see thousands of "little animals" going about their lives. Over time, more and more single-celled microbes were discovered living in different parts of the human body—covering our skin, crowding into our belly buttons, and colonizing our mouth, nose, and intestines.

At first, every microbe found in our bodies was thought of as a "germ"—something that could cause disease. But only a few kinds of microbes threaten human health. We have discovered many more that help keep our bodies working properly.

They do this by:
- Making substances, including vitamins and proteins, that our own cells don't know how to make.
- Breaking down foods that our own cells can't digest.
- Boosting our immune system.
- Keeping harmful microbes and other invaders at bay.

Body microbiome

Together, these helpful, "friendly" microbes are known as our "microbiome." This giant community of cells is so important that many scientists now think of it as one of our organs! They are finding links between our microbiome and every area of health, from how well we can fight disease to how happy we feel. Microbes are an essential part of every healthy human.

Microbe cells are often much smaller than human cells. But together, the microbes living in your body weigh more than your brain.

Yeast cell
Scientific name: *Candida albicans*
Location: on your skin

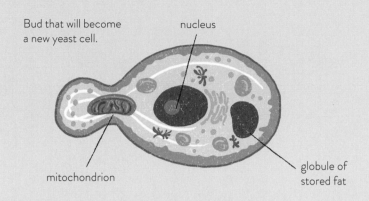

Bud that will become a new yeast cell.

nucleus

mitochondrion

globule of stored fat

4 micrometers

Bacterial cells
Scientific name: *Lactobacillus*
Location: in your mouth

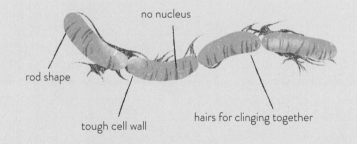

no nucleus

rod shape

tough cell wall

hairs for clinging together

up to 6 micrometers long

Protozoan cell
Scientific name: *Dientamoeba fragilis*
Location: in your large intestine

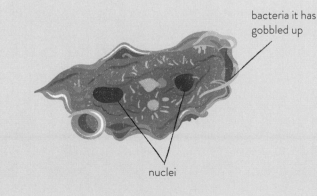

bacteria it has gobbled up

nuclei

10–20 micrometers

57

THE GARDEN IN YOUR GUT

Most of the microbes that make up your microbiome are found inside your intestines. This is a great place for them to find food. Every time you eat, you are feeding billions of tiny creatures too.

A newborn baby is a microbe-free zone, but friendly microbes begin to move in and multiply within hours. They come from everything we touch, lick, eat, and drink. By the time we are adults, we have collected more bacteria cells in our gut than there are stars in the Milky Way. Most of these microbes are not dangerous invaders. They are an important part of our digestive and immune systems.

A healthy human gut is often home to thousands of different types of microbes. In return for snacking on our food, the microbes help break down certain substances and build vitamins we can't make ourselves—such as vitamin B12 and vitamin K. They also protect us from harmful invaders by using up so much of the space and resources in your gut that dangerous microbes get crowded out.

This is why our immune system ignores the friendly microbes in our guts and may even help to protect them. For a long time, doctors thought our appendix—a finger-shaped pouch in our large intestine—did nothing at all. Scientists now think that it might provide a safe hiding place for friendly bacteria when we have a stomach bug.

Gut bacteria
Scientific name: *Bacteroides fragilis*
Location: in your large intestine

friendly when it
stays in your gut

rod-shaped

can cause disease if it
gets into your blood

can live without
oxygen

up to 6 micrometers long

These discoveries are helping us invent new ways of treating illnesses. For example, we may be able to treat an infection of "bad" bacteria by adding more "friendly" bacteria to crowd them out. Doctors are already treating certain conditions by transplanting poop (and microbes) from the intestines of healthy people to the intestines of patients. This could be healthier than taking antibiotics, which kill harmful bacteria but also kill the friendly bacteria we need to stay healthy.

There are lots of questions
left to answer about our
30 trillion or more
microbe cells.

If we learn how to **take care of them** better,
they will **take care of us better too!**

YOU AND YOUR CELLS

You are an amazing team: a community of 30 trillion human cells and at least 30 trillion microbe cells, all working together to form one awesome human being.

Your cells are the building blocks of your body, but they are also much more. In each of your 30 trillion cells—a speck too tiny to see with your eyes—hundreds or thousands of chemical reactions are happening at once. Substances are broken down. New substances are built and stored. It is your cells that carry out the chemistry of life.

Instead of trying to do everything for themselves, your cells split the work between them. Each cell has its own identity—a certain shape, size, and set of tasks that allow it to play its part in your body. Together, groups of cells form tissues, organs, and body systems, each one more complex than the last.

By understanding what happens inside cells—and how they work together—we can explain how our bodies move, breathe, feed, feel, see, hear, grow, and reproduce. We can also begin to explain how we think and learn, why we feel happy or sad, why we sometimes get sick, and why we age.

Sixty trillion
incredible cells form one of
the most complex things in
the entire universe
—you!

GLOSSARY

antibody: a protein made by the body, to help the body recognise and destroy harmful substances more quickly.

atom: tiny building blocks that make all matter.

bacteria: tiny living organisms, each a single cell. Some are essential for our health and others cause disease.

billion: one thousand millions (1,000,000,000).

calcium: a metal essential for bones, teeth and many processes in the body. Common sources are dairy products and some leafy, green vegetables.

capillary: the tiniest blood vessels.

carbon dioxide: a gas in the air that the body produces and breathes out.

cell: the smallest working part of a living thing.

chemical: any substance that is unique and has a name, from water to carbon dioxide to bleach to DNA.

chemical reaction: a process that results in the structure of one or more substances being changed, creating new substances.

chromosomes: threadlike structures inside the nucleus of complex cells, made up of tightly coiled DNA and other proteins.

cytoplasm: a goo made of water, salts and proteins that fills cells.

DNA: Stands for deoxyribonucleic acid, a chemical with large molecules that is found in almost every living cell, and which carries the coded information that tells each cell how to work.

enzyme: a protein that acts as a natural catalyst, starting, speeding up, or carrying out chemical reactions in living things.

fiber: a long, thin threadlike structure, for example muscle fibers or nerve fibers.

gene: a short section of DNA that carries coded information relating to a particular characteristic of that living thing.

genome: the total genetic information carried inside every living thing

germ: a microbe or virus capable of infecting a living thing and causing harm.

hormones: chemical messengers that trigger certain cells or tissues to do something.

lipids: fats and similar substances in the body.

membrane: a very thin sheet that forms a barrier, such as the membrane around cells.

microbe: a tiny living organism, only visible under a microscope, such as a bacterium.

micrometer: a unit of measurement; there are one thousand micrometers in one millimeter.

minerals: non-living substance found in nature, made from a particular set of elements. Living things need to absorb or ingest certain minerals to survive.

mitochondria: the power stations in cells that break down fats and sugars to release energy.

molecule: two or more atoms joined together.

mucus: a sticky substance made in the body to protect parts of it.

nerve: a bundle of nerve fibers that carries electrical messages to and from the brain and spinal cord and the rest of the body.

nucleus: a cell's control center. It contains the instructions for the cell.

nutrients: substances that living things need to grow and thrive.

organ: a specialized part of the body that does a particular job, such as the brain or heart.

organism: an individual living thing.

organelle: a cell.

oxygen: a gas essential for life. We breathe it in from the air, and our blood moves it all around our bodies.

pigment: a substance that gives something its color.

plasma: the liquid substance that blood cells are carried in.

protein: a complex molecule made by a living thing, which does certain jobs inside that living thing.

tissue: a collection of the same type of cells, such as muscle or bone tissue.

transplant: to replace something in someone's body that is no longer working, for example a heart.

trillion: one thousand billion (1,000,000,000,000).

UV (ultraviolet) rays: the part of sunlight that can damage skin and eyes.

virus: the smallest and simplest germs, each made up of genetic information wrapped in a protective coat.

vitamins: substances needed by living things for good health. People normally get their vitamins from food.

INDEX

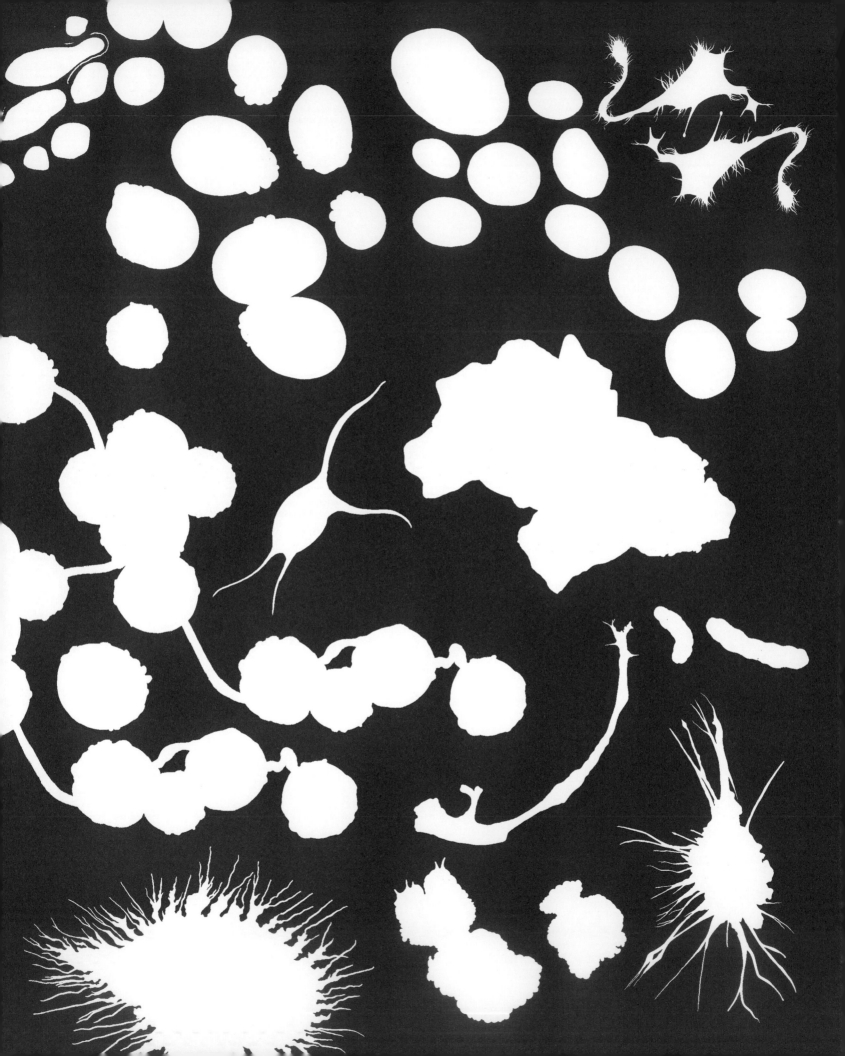